Jeffrey Plowman

CAMOUFLAGE & MARKINGS

of the

VALENTINES

in
New Zealand
Service

Model Centrum PROGRES   www.modelbooks.republika.pl

Armor Color Gallery #10

Camouflage & Markings of the
Valentines
in New Zealand Service

Jeffrey Plowman

Published by Model Centrum Progres, Poland
Warsaw, June 2012

ISBN 978-83-60672-19-8

Edited by Wojciech J. Gawrych
Cover layout, design and layout by
PROGRES Publishing House, Warsaw
DTP and prepress by AIRES-GRAF, Warsaw
Printed and bound in European Union by
Regis Ltd., Napoleona 4, 05-230 Kobyłka, Poland

First Edition

Exclusive Distributor
International Business Group
ul. B. Hertza 2,
04-603 Warsaw, Poland
fax +48 22 8159151
ibgsc@ibg.com.pl
www.ibg.com.pl

Contents

Acknowledgements 3

Introduction 4

NZAFV School 5

1st NZ Army Tank Brigade 6

    Brigade HQ Squadron 6

    1st Army Tank Battalion 9

    2nd Army Tank Battalion 12

    3rd Army Tank Battalion 13

3rd NZ Division Special Army Tank Squadron Group 17

Mounted Rifle Regiments 27

2nd NZ Division 28

School of Armor 29

Royal NZ Armored Corps 31

Color Plates 35

Acknowledgments

I wish to thank the following people for help with this book, in particular the veterans and family members cited in the captions who kindly loaned me photographs: E. Anderson, George Andrews, Jim Becker, Les Brooker, Peter Brown, Frank Bulling, Alan Burgess, Tom Evans, Ruth French, Eric Goodwin, George Hodgson, George Kerr, Shane Lovell, Doug McGlashan, Don McKay, Penn McKay, Mark McKenzie, John McKim, Molly Middlemiss, Stratton Morrin, J. Neal, Dick Otway, George Pearson, Mark Priestly, Les Pye, D. Robinson, Jim Rutherford, Mike Starmer, Doug Sibbald, Glen Sibbald, Malcolm Thomas and Lance Whitford. In addition I would like to thank the following organizations: the Alexander Turnbull Library, Archives New Zealand, the Auckland Institute and Museum, the U.S. National Archives and Records Administration (NARA), the National Army Museum (NZ), the New Zealand Army, the Museum of Transport and Technology, the Royal New Zealand Armored Corps and Tesla Studios.

ARMOR COLOR GALLERY

A column of Valentines from B Squadron, 3rd Armored Regiment taking part in a parade along Dee Street, Invercargill in the early 1950s. The tanks are all completed in overall Bronze Green, while the B Squadron square would be blue. They appear to have been given names of towns from the Italian campaign; the lead Valentine V (NZ13902) being named "Florence", while the Valentine V (NZ13903) following carried the name "Rimini". [R. French]

The Valentine tank arrived in New Zealand as a result of efforts by General Sir Bernard Freyberg, commander of the 2nd New Zealand Division, to obtain armored support for his troops in Egypt. Freyberg had approached the Middle East high command in October 1940 to ask for enough cruiser tanks to equip a tank battalion, with the view to incorporating it into an armored brigade that was also to include the Divisional Cavalry Regiment, 27 Machine Gun Battalion and a battalion of infantry. While General Wavell (C in C of the Middle East) appeared to be sympathetic to Freyberg's needs, the British War Office were not and, instead, they felt that New Zealand should consider this a longer term project. As a result the New Zealand Government agreed to a visit from a British advisor on armored warfare, General Sir Guy Williams, which took place in May 1941. At the conclusion of his visit one of Williams' main recommendations was for New Zealand to form a school for the instruction of armored fighting vehicles, a move that would entitle the Army to some 40 tanks from the UK. While these were primarily intended for training purposes they would also help bolster the country's defense forces in the event that it was threatened by invasion. In turn, New Zealand would have to agree to raise a tank brigade for eventual deployment in the Middle East. It was as a result of these discussions that the Prime Minister Peter Fraser gave his approval for the training of the necessary instructors in the Middle East and, with Freyberg's agreement, a number of personnel were drawn off from the 2nd NZEF and sent to the Middle East armored training school at Abbassia in Egypt.

NZAFV School

At the beginning of August 1941 the officers, their training at Abbassia complete, returned to New Zealand where they established the New Zealand Armored Fighting Vehicles (NZAFV) School at Waiouru Military Camp in the central North Island. Lacking any tanks for training, the school had to fall back on Bren gun carriers, lorries and even spare engines until the first 10 Valentine IIs arrived in Wellington in October. A further 10 were shipped in the following month, followed by another 10 in December, with the balance of the promised 40 tanks being received in April 1942. These Valentines were handed over to the 1st NZ Army Tank Brigade but later, when more were received, a number were issued to the NZAFV School and were augmented by Mark IIIs and Vs when these arrived.

Because it was located at Waiouru Military Camp the NZAFV School was part of the Army Headquarters Reserve hence all their vehicles, like this Valentine V (T-66612) carried its A insignia, in addition to their serial number 35, both in a black square. Later shipments of tanks from England, including this tank, would have been completed in overall Dark Brown. It is still carrying its War Department serial on the driver's hatch. [M. Priestly]

Among the first Valentines received by the New Zealand Army was this Valentine II, "Ellason" which was issued to the NZAFV School. It still carries a shipping mark on the front plate and, like the first Valentines received by New Zealand, would have been finished in overall Dark Green. [G. Hodgson]

The 1st NZ Army Tank Brigade came into being in September 1941 when an intake of officers and NCOs were marched into Waiouru Military Camp, some having come from the 2nd NZ Division in the Middle East, the rest being drawn from Territorial Force personnel within New Zealand. These men were divided up into the three battalions of the new unit, the Brigade Headquarters squadron and associated support units. The plan was to train it in the country and then return it to the Middle East early in 1942. Unfortunately, the Japanese attack on Pearl Harbor ended these plans, the government having no option but to retain it in the country as an essential part of its defense forces. As a result they decided to bring it up to full strength and purchase enough tanks for the brigade as well as provide it with an operational reserve of 80%. Thus shipments of Valentines resumed within weeks of the last of the promised 40 arriving, initially of the AEC diesel-engined Mk II, but later some Mk IIIs started to arrive, the latter selected by the Army for its three-man turret and because it had the same engine. This plan went somewhat awry, though, when the first Valentine Bridgelayers arrived in the country and the Army discovered that they had GMC diesel engine, forcing them to complete their purchase order of Valentines with Mk Vs.

At the outbreak of war with Japan, the 30 Valentines in the country were handed over to the Tank Brigade, who used them to equip an emergency tank battalion drawn from all elements of the brigade. Later these were issued to the 3rd Army Tank Battalion, the first to be brought up to full strength when shipments of Valentines resumed. Thus equipped each tank battalion was organized along the lines of a Regimental Headquarters of four tanks and three squadrons each with a Squadron Headquarters of four tanks and five troops of three tanks each. In the early stages of the brigade's existence the only tanks on issue were Mk IIs but with the arrival of the Mk IIIs and Mk Vs it was possible to reorganize each troop so that the troop leader had a three-man turreted tank, while the other two tanks were the two-man turreted Mk IIs.

The brigade was eventually broken up at the end of 1942 and the 3rd Army Tank Battalion sent to the Middle East as reinforcements for the newly formed 4th NZ Armored Brigade. Of the other units, the Brigade Headquarters Squadron was transferred to the South Island to bolster their defense forces, while the 1st Army Tank Battalion remained an army tank unit, keeping all its Valentines, and was moved up to Helvetia Camp near Auckland to replace the 3rd Army Tank Battalion that had been stationed there. The 2nd Army Tank Battalion, however, was reorganized as an armored regiment, with A and B Squadrons receiving Stuarts while C Squadron retained their Valentines. All three units were eventually disbanded in June 1943 and the bulk of their personnel dispatched to the Middle East.

Brigade HQ Squadron

A Valentine II (NZ16556) "Sphakia" from the Brigade HQ Squadron pushing over a tree at Harewood camp. It is completed in a two-tone scheme of Dark Green and Dark Earth. The rampant dragon insignia of the 1st NZ Army Tank Brigade is in a black square and the 20 in a brown square. [D. Sibbald]

This Valentine V (NZ13892) from the Brigade HQ Squadron became stuck during an exercise near Harewood. It is completed in a two-tone scheme of Dark Green and Dark Earth. The rampant dragon insignia of the 1st NZ Army Tank Brigade is in a black square and the 20 in a brown square, while it carries the name "Lamia", a town in Greece, the unit having adopted names from the Mediterranean Theatre of operations. [D. Sibbald]

[Left & below left] In 1943 the Brigade Headquarters Squadron moved to a camp near Harewood airfield outside Christchurch in the South Island. This Mark V (NZ13899) was photographed netting in at their camp one morning. It is completed in a two-tone scheme of Dark Green and Dark Earth. The dragon insignia was in a black square while the unit serial 20 was in a brown square. The tactical marking on the turret consists of the number 2 inside a single-pointed pennant. [D. Sibbald]

A Valentine II (NZ16524) "Servia" from the Brigade HQ Squadron during an exercise in 1943. It is completed in the Dark Green and Dark Earth scheme of the unit, the dragon being in a black square and the unit serial 20 would be in a brown square. At least two versions of Dragon appeared to be in use by the Tank Brigade, this being the more stylized of the two. [D. Sibbald]

Just before the Brigade Headquarters Squadron was disbanded in June 1943 it took part in a parade in Dunedin, this Valentine V (NZ13905, "Sidi Barrani") being photographed driving down Cumberland Street. Like all tanks from the unit it is completed in the two-tone scheme of Dark Green and Dark Earth, with the dragon in a black square and the unit serial in a brown square. Its turret marking consists of a 4 inside a triangular pennant. [M. Middlemiss]

Moving Valentine tanks around New Zealand proved to be something of a problem because of the narrow gauge of the local railways. The Army overcame this by attaching sleeper to Ub-flat railway wagons. The tank were then driven on at one end i the manner shown here by this Va entine II (NZ16460) from the Brigad Headquarters Squadron. This tan is completed in a two-tone disrup tive scheme of Dark Earth over Dar Green, while the unit serial 20 on th rear plate was in a brown square. The number 5 on the turret appears to b part of the tactical marking scheme the unit, which appeared to involv different styles of pennants. [Nationa Army Museum]

1st Army Tank Battalion

Repairs in the field for a tank from 7 Troop, 1st Army Tank Battalio at Waiouru. The name possibly i "Ngangau". The unit serial 21 on the rear plate is in a red square.

After the break up of the Tank Brigad in December 1942, newly forme 1 Tanks Battalion Group moved t Helvetia Camp. Here Valentines from 2 Troop, A Squadron were photo graphed on a west coast beach nea the camp. They are from left to right: Valentine II, "Karatane"; a Valentin V, "Koehu" (the white troop numbe indicating that it is the troop leader' tank), and a Valentine II, "Kiriri". [M Priestly]

Three views of a Valentine II from 2 Troop, A Squadron, 1st Army Tank Battalion, the first view showing it during manoeuvres in the Waiouru training area in 1942. It is completed in the Brigade scheme of Dark Earth over Dark Green. Like other tanks in the unit they carried their A Squadron triangle and troop number, both in red, on both sides of the turret and in between the unit serial 21 in a red square and the Army Headquarters Reserve "A" insignia in a black square. [M. Priestly]

On one occasion its crew was photographed replacing a track in the mud. [M. Priestly]

While later it was photographed being hauled out of a hole. [J. Plowman]

A Valentine II (T-32736) "Ngara" of
7 Troop, B Squadron, 1st Army Tank
Battalion at Waiouru Camp in 1942.
The vehicle was in a three-tone
scheme of Dark Green over-painted
with stripes of Dark Earth and Khaki
Green. The unit insignia was 21 in a
red square on the right side and the
letter A on the left side. The B Squadron square and troop number on the
turret were red. [L. Whitford]

Crewmen from 1 Tanks Battalion
Group on a beach near Helvetia Camp
pulling back the gun of a Valentine V
to exercise its recoil system and
check for its proper operation. The
tank is from 2 Troop, C Squadron and
is completed in Dark Green and Dark
Earth. The Dragon was in a black
square and the 21 in a red square.
This is the second style of Dragon,
the head, body and upper part of the
wings being noticeably thinner than
the other. [M. Priestly]

2nd Army Tank Battalion

A Valentine III (T-59800) of 8 Troop of B Squadron, 2nd Army Tank Battalion stopped in full view of Mount Ruapehu in 1942. It appears to be completed in overall S.C.C. 2 Brown. The B Squadron square on the turret is yellow, while the troop number is white, indicating that this is a troop leader's tank. It still carries its War Department serial number T-59800 on the driver's hatch. [F. Bulling]

A Valentine III from RHQ of the 2nd Army Tank Battalion in Waiouru Camp in 1942. It is completed in a two-tone scheme of Dark Green with stripes of S.C.C. 2 Brown with the unit serial 22 on a yellow square on the left side of the front plate, while the yellow RHQ diamond was on the front plate and the turret. The white number 1 indicates that this is the regimental commander's tank. [F. Bulling]

A Valentine III from 13 troop, C Squadron, 2 Tanks Battalion Group on a Federal tank transporter, during a parade in Auckland in June 1943. It is completed in a two-tone scheme of Dark Green and Dark Earth and carries its new unit serial 26 in a yellow square on the left side of the front plate. The yellow C Squadron circle is on the turret side as well as the center of the front plate, while the troop number is white, indicating that this was a troop leader's tank. [Alexander Turnbull Library]

Valentine IIs from 3rd Army Tank Battalion outside their barracks in Waiouru Camp in 1942. They are finished in a two-tone scheme of Dark Green and Dark Earth. The unit serial 23 and A insignia appear to be painted directly onto the front plate. [A. Burgess]

Valentine IIs from A Squadron, 3rd Army Tank Battalion lined up on a beach near Helvetia Camp in 1942. They are finished in a two-tone scheme of Dark Green and Dark Earth. The unit serial 23 is in a green square, while the green A Squadron triangle was outlined in white. The Army serial of the tanks are from left to right: NZ16515, NZ16550, NZ16483 and NZ16489. [J. Becker]

A Valentine II from 9 Troop, B Squadron, 3rd Army Tank Battalion taking part in a United Nations Day parade in Auckland in June 1942. It appears to be completed in a two-tone scheme of Dark Green and Dark Earth. The unit serial 23 is in a green square and the A symbol of Army Headquarters Reserve in a black square. The B Squadron square and troop number were also green, necessitating the former being outlined in white to make it more visible. [S. Morrin]

Two photos of a Valentine II from B Squadron, 3rd Army Tank Battalion during manoeuvres in the hills around Pukekohe in 1942. The unit serial and A insignia were painted directly onto the tank while the green B Squadron square was outlined in white. It appears to be completed in overall S.C.C. 2 Brown. Some of the Valentines with it appear to have individual numbers inside their squadron insignia, 10 on the rear of the tank to the left and 4 on the turret of the tank to the right. [D. Robinson]

A Valentine II from A Squadron, 3r Army Tank Battalion out in the fiel at Waiouru in 1942. It is complete in a two-tone scheme of Dark Gree and Dark Earth. The unit serial 23 i in a green square and the A insigni in a black square, while the gree A Squadron triangle on the turret wa outlined in white to make it more vis ible. [E. R. Otway]

A Valentine II from A Squadron, 3r Army Tank Battalion towing a lengt of track in sand hill country near Hel vetia Camp in 1942. It is finished in two-tone scheme of Dark Green an Dark Earth. It carries on the rear plat the unit serial 23 in a green square a green A Squadron triangle outline in white and a Rampant Dragon in black square. [J. Becker]

A Valentine II from C Squadron, 3r Army Tank Battalion out in the fiel near Helvetia Camp in 1942. The tan is completed in a two-tone scheme o Dark Green and Dark Earth. The uni serial 23 is in a green square and A insignia in a black square, while th green C Squadron circle on the turre was outlined in white. [E. Goodwin]

A Valentine II from 3rd Army Tank Battalion on the road near Helvetia Camp in Pukekohe in 1942. The tank, from 7 Troop, B Squadron, is completed in a two-tone scheme of Dark Green and Dark Earth. The unit serial 23 is in a green square and the A insignia in a black square appear to be painted directly onto the camouflaged front plate, while the green B Squadron square is outlined in white. [Museum of Transport and Technology]

A Valentine II of A Squadron, 3rd Army Tank Battalion backing off a Jib-flat wagon at Pukekohe in July 1942. The vehicle is completed in a two-tone camouflage scheme of Dark Green over-painted with Dark Earth stripes. Its green A Squadron triangle is outlined in white, while the A insignia and unit serial 23 appear to have been painted directly onto the camouflage on the rear plate. [R. Eastgate]

3rd NZ Division Special Army Tank Squadron Group

In 1942 it had become apparent to the New Zealand government that there was a need for them to deploy a division-sized force in the Pacific Theatre of operations. As a result the Army raised a two-brigade unit that was to become the 3rd NZ Division and for armored support they set aside the 2nd Army Tank Battalion at Waiouru. By June 1943, however, the Army came to the realization that realistically all they could deploy was a squadron-sized tank force with the Division so the battalion was disbanded and the bulk of its personnel posted to the Middle East. The remaining men were formed into the 3rd NZ Division Special Army Tank Squadron Group, an autonomous unit, having its own support elements and equipped with Valentine IIIs. Prior to their departure the lack of high explosive capability in the Valentine was overcome in two ways, one by developing a high explosive and canister round for their 2-pounders and also by converting a number of them to a close-support version by replacing their 2-pounders with 3-inch howitzers from Matilda IV CS tanks. A total of 18 of close support Valentine IIIs were converted to the CS version, nine of which were issued to the squadron, while the other nine were retained in New Zealand as an operational reserve. The squadron was organized along the lines of a Squadron Headquarters with two Valentine III CS tanks and two standard Valentine IIIs and five troops of three tanks, one of which was a Valentine III CS.

Major Rutherford's Valentine III CS tank from Squadron Headquarters in the Guadalcanal jungle in October 1943. The diamond is yellow, while the number inside is white. [L. Brooker]

The Tank Squadron was shipped to the Pacific in August 1943, initially to Guadalcanal in the Solomons Islands where they trained with the 8th NZ Brigade. Plans to send them to the Treasuries, further north in the Solomons Group with this unit were thwarted by lack of shipping, however in February 1944 they were detailed to support the 15th NZ Brigade in its attack on the Green Island Group at the northwestern end of the Solomons. Even then transport shortages meant that only half the squadron could accompany the first wave and in the end 1 and 3 Troops and the two Valentine III CS tanks from SHQ were selected. They landed on Nissan Island on 15 February and spent the next few days assisting the infantry in searching for the Japanese garrison, the last remnants of which were discovered near the village of Tanaheran on 20 February by the Brigade Carrier Squadron. They and the tanks then became involved in a pitched battle with this Japanese force until reinforced by a company of infantry from 30th Battalion. This was the first and only engagement fought by the Tank Squadron. Manpower shortages in New Zealand forced the gradual stripping of personnel from all ground forces in the Pacific over the next few months until they were all brought back to New Zealand and disbanded.

Major Rutherford's Valentine III CS tank backing into a Landing Ship Tank on Kukum Beach, Guadalcanal, on 11 February 1944. The Squadron headquarters diamond was yellow and the number 1 white. Operations in the jungle soon led to the lower parts of the tanks getting covered in mud resulting which obscured the unit insignia, apart from the dragon just visible on the front plate. [R. J. Rutherford]

Valentine IIIs of 1 Troop on Kukum Beach, Guadalcanal, on 11 February 1944 waiting their turn to embark on a LST for Nissan Island. Note the unit insignia on the rear plate, from left to right: the Dragon, Kiwi and unit serial 26. [T. K. Evans]

A Valentine III from of 1 Troop backing onto LST 447 on Kukum beach, Guadalcanal on 11 February 1944. [T. K. Evans]

The Squadron's Second in Command's Valentine III CS coming ashore on Nissan Island on the 15th of February. The tank is completed in the squadron's three-tone scheme: base color Khaki Green, over-painted with Dark Green and over-sprayed with spots of Lime Green. The tactical insignia on the front plate: 26 in a yellow square, Kiwi in a black square, white 2 in a yellow diamond and Rampant Dragon in a black square (this being the more basic style of Dragon applied only to the Valentine III CS tanks). The white 2 in a yellow diamond was also carried on the forward part of the turret. [E. R. Otway]

[Above] One of the Valentine IIIs from 3 Troop coming ashore on Red Beach, Nissan Island, on 15 February 1944, a US 90 mm anti-aircraft gun behind it under tow. This is believed to be the Troop Sergeant's tank. [Alexander Turnbull Library]

[Below] Engineers conducting a bridging exercise at Trentham Camp in September 1944. The Valentine III CS crossing it was one of the nine converted after the 3rd Division Tank Squadron departed for New Caledonia and was to act as a replacement for any losses in action. It is completed in quite an intricate three-tone disruptive scheme, possibly of Dark Green, Khaki Green and Lime Green. [Alexander Turnbull Library]

Native tribesmen from Nissan Island gather to view the Troop Sergeant's tank from 3 Troop after it had come to a halt in the Tangalan Plantation. The Lime Green spots of its camouflage pattern are clearly visible here. [T. K. Evans]

A frontal view of the 3 Troop Sergeant's Valentine III in the Tangalan Plantation. Though the lower part of the tank is covered in mud the Lime Green spots of its camouflage pattern are evident as is the upper layer of darker green. [Alexander Turnbull Library]

The 3 Troop Sergeant's Valentine I entering the Tangalan Plantation o 15 February 1944 still towing its US 90 mm anti-aircraft gun. It is com pleted in the three-tone scheme: base color Khaki Green, over-painted wit Dark Green and over-sprayed with spots of Lime Green. Visible on th rear plate are some of the unit's tacti cal markings: a Kiwi in a black square and the unit serial 26 in a yellow square. The troop number in yellow was carried on the sides of the turret and Bren ammunition box on the tu ret rear. [L. F. Brooker]

A line of Valentines from 1 Troop i the jungle on Nissan Island, the troo marking visible on the Bren ammuni tion box on the turret of the neares tank. This troop was noticeable fo fitting a Stuart grouser box on the lef rear track-guard. On the right of the POW rack on the tank-infantry tel ephone box is the lettering TL, whic stood for troop leader, indicating tha this was Lieutenant Tom Evan's Val entine III CS. [L. F. Brooker]

[Above] A Valentine III halted during the advance through the jungle of Nissan Island. Though covered in mud the unit serial 26 and Dragon insignia can just be made out on the front plate. [NARA]

[Below] Valentine IIIs of the squadron advancing through the jungle of Nissan Island in February 1944. To the right of the rack for the petrol oil/water cans is an ammunition box converted to hold their infantry-tank telephone. The markings on the rear plate consist of the Dragon insignia on the left and the Kiwi and unit serial 26 on the right. [NARA]

Valentines of 3 Troop advancing along the beach from South Point, on 18 February 1944, the tank in the foreground most likely being the troop sergeant's tank. As a result of their advance through the surf the mud has washed off revealing their full set of hull front markings, consisting of the unit serial 26, the Kiwi, the 3 Troop insignia and the Rampant Dragon. [NZ Army]

Vehicles of the 3rd NZ Division Tank Squadron halted on the road between Nepoi and Moindah, in New Caledonia. The nearest vehicle is a Valentine III CS and carries the standard unit markings on the rear plate. Note that this Dragon is of a different style to the 2iC's Valentine III CS, it has the simpler head but the wing is bigger where it joins onto the body. [L. F. Brooker]

A Valentine III from 2 Troop at their camp at Salipal on Nissan Island after the cessation of hostilities in February 1944. Note the troop number II on the turret side. [National Archives]

Mounted Rifle Regiments

In 1942 the Army converted the nine mounted rifle regiments to light armored fighting vehicles (LAFV) regiments, initially equipping them with a mixture of locally produced Beaverette Scout Cars and Universal Carriers, the former in lieu of light tanks which did not start to arrive in quantity until September 1942. Shortly afterwards the armored force in New Zealand was reorganized and two mounted rifle regiments in each of Northern and Central Military Districts and one in Southern Military District converted to armored regiments, on the basis of two squadrons of Stuarts and one of Valentines. They continued in this form until June 1943 when most were reduced to cadre strength and the bulk of their personnel sent over to the Middle East to provide reinforcements for the 2nd NZ Division.

A Valentine II of C Squadron, 5th Otago Mounted Rifles (Armored) at the Wingatui Racecourse in 1943. The tank would have been completed in S.C.C. 2 Brown. The only markings visible are the green C Squadron circle on the turret side and the Kea's head insignia of the 5th Division on the front plate. The latter would have been inside a yellow square. [D. McKay]

A line of tanks headed by a Valentine V from C Squadron, 9th Wellington East Coast Mounted Rifles (Armored) advancing up the escarpment on the Desert Road, north of Waiouru in March 1943. The tank would have been completed in overall S.C.C. 2 Brown. The only thing visible in this view is the unit serial 3 on the front plate, which would have been in a green square. The charging water buffalo insignia in its red square on the other side has been obscured by dust. The C Squadron circle would have been green. [R. J. McGlashan]

2nd NZ Division

A number of Valentine Bridgelayers were on the strength of the 2nd NZ Division. There were several on issue to the 4th Armored Brigade Headquarters and these saw extensive service from the time the Division landed in Italy in late 1943 until the end of the war. Prior to the launch of the final offensive over the Senio River in April 1945 a special unit was formed within the Divisional Engineers the 28th Assault Squadron. This unit was equipped with a variety of armored vehicles among them Sherman Fascine carriers, Arks and bulldozers and included some Valentine Bridgelayers.

A Valentine bridge-layer of the 28th NZ Assault Squadron crossing a Sherman Ark, also from the Squadron. It would have been camouflaged in the overall Olive Drab. It carries a type of distinguishing insignia peculiar to the unit, consisting of the letters T5 inside a square, these possibly finished in white. [C. N. Bosher]

This Valentine Bridgelayer of the 4th NZ Armored Brigade Headquarters ended up in one of the craters along Route 6 while unsuccessfully trying to recover a scissors bridge along Route 6 at Cassino in March 1944. It appears to have been camouflaged in the standard scheme of the time of S.C.C. 14 Light Mud and Blue-black. It carries the combined divisional insignia (the Silver Fern) and unit serial patch (65 in a red square) in the center of the front plate. [G. R. Andrews]

School of Armor

In 1949 the NZAFV School was reactivated at Waiouru and renamed the School of Armor. It retained on strength a number of Valentines to train the new recruits in the Territorial Force armored units. Among the Valentines on strength were Mark IIs, a Mark III CS and a Mark V.

The commander of a Valentine III CS (NZ23934) observing the fall of shot in the Waiouru training area. The tank was part of a special squadron formed by the Royal NZ Armored Corps in 1949 for Exercise "Tally Ho", the first one conducted after World War II by armor in New Zealand. The vehicle would have been completed in overall Bronze Green. It carries a white 12 in a light gray square on the right of the rear plate alongside its Army registration number, which was also painted on a tool box on the track-guard. On the turret side is the vertically divided red-and-yellow A Squadron triangle. [M. Priestly]

A Valentine III (NZ21648) moving at speed through the tussock at Waiouru during Exercise "Tally Ho" in 1949. Completed in overall Bronze Green, it carries a white 12 in a light gray square on the left of the front plate and the vertically divided red-and-yellow A Squadron triangle on the turret side. [M. Priestly]

A Valentine V (NZ20742) during a practice shoot on the ranges at Waiouru. Completed in overall Bronze Green, it carries a white 12 in a light gray square on the left of the front plate, its NZ number on the muffler cover and the vertically divided red-and-yellow A Squadron triangle on the turret side and rear. [M. Priestly]

The crew of a Valentine V (NZ20762) of the School of Armor at Waiouru in the 1950s in the process of repairing the gun trunnions. The vehicle is completed in overall Bronze Green. The tactical insignia consists of a white 12 in a light gray square and an A Squadron triangle divided vertically red and yellow on the front plate. This A Squadron insignia is repeated on the turret side, while the NZ-number can be seen on the side locker. [M. Priestly]

Above right] A Valentine III CS of the School of Armor in the field at Waiouru in the 1950s. It is completed in overall Bronze Green and carries a white 12 in a light gray square on the front plate alongside the vertically divided red and yellow A Squadron triangle, the latter also being found on the turret sides. [L. Pye]

A line up of Valentines (including, from front to back, one Mk V, two Mk IIs and one Mk III CS) undergoing routine servicing outside the School of Armor at Waiouru in the 1950s. Completed in overall Bronze Green, their markings consist of the red-and-yellow triangle on the right side of the front plate, a white 12 in a gray square on the left side. The red-and-yellow triangle was also painted on both sides of the turret. They all carry their NZ-army registration number on the cover over the muffler. The tank in foreground NZ20740 is a Mark V, while the Mark II behind it is Z16489. [Royal NZ Armored Corps]

In 1950 the Territorial Force of the Army was re-activated as a result of the New Zealand government announcing its intention to raise a division from its territorial units in case it was needed for service overseas. To provide personnel for this unit the government of the day re-introduced a compulsory military training scheme. The New Zealand Division was based around a structure of three infantry brigades with ancillary artillery, engineer and army service units. In addition division was to have an armored brigade, its personnel to be drawn from the former mounted rifle regiments, which by this time had been reduced to squadron-sized units in an armored regiment in each military district. As no new tanks had been purchased since the war they were equipped with one squadron of Stuarts and two of Valentines. The Stuarts were phased out sometime around 1956 but the Valentines remained in service with the Regular Force of the New Zealand Army until 1960 when they were replaced by the US M41 Walker Bulldog. This was not the end of its Army life as, after its retirement, some were handed over to the Territorial Force units for training these troops in their home areas.

[Below left] A Valentine III (NZ14025 of C Squadron, 3rd Armored Regiment halted in Burkes Pass while moving up to their annual camp at Tekapo in 1955. The unit serial 64 i in a horizontally divided red over yellow square on the front plate and carries the white lettering 4B inside a blue C Squadron circle, the former presumably for vehicle or troop identification. At this stage the unit serial of the rest of the 4th Armored Brigade were: Headquarters 4th Armored Brigade – 58; 1st Armored Regiment 59; 2nd Armored Regiment – 63. [P McKay]

Valentines on manoeuvres at Waiouru in the 1950s. While the 3rd Armored Regiment in the South Island carried their unit serial number on their tanks it was not possible to do this in the North Island as the two (and later three) armored units had to share pool of vehicles based at Waiouru. Instead, like this Valentine, they just added temporary tactical marking on the turret. Note that it still has the red/yellow divided triangle o the hull front, though the number 1 in its gray square has been covered over with a darker colored square. The tanks would all have been completed in overall Bronze Green. [M Priestly]

Valentine V from 3 Troop, C Squadron, 3rd Armored Regiment taking part in a shoot over the river upstream from Balmoral Camp at Tekapo in 1955. Finished in overall Bronze Green, it carries the lettering B in white inside a blue C Squadron circle. [P. McKay]

Valentine V (NZ13901) of 3 Troop, C Squadron, 3rd Armored Regiment at the Tekapo training area in 1955. It carries its arm of service insignia consisting of the number 64 in a horizontally divided red-over-yellow square on the hull front plate next to the NZ number, while the tank number 3 was painted in inside the B Squadron square. It would be completed in overall Bronze Green. [P. McKay]

Above right] A Valentine V (NZ13902) of 2 Troop, B Squadron, 3rd Armored Regiment at the Tekapo training area in 1955. It carries the unit serial 64 in a horizontally divided red-over-yellow square on the hull front plate next to the NZ number, while the tank number 2 was painted in white inside a white outlined square (though note the colored square in front of it, most probably blue). It was completed in overall Bronze Green. [P. McKay]

Valentine V (NZ15215) of 3 Troop, C Squadron, 3rd Armored Regiment during the unit's annual camp at Lake Rotoiti in 1953. The arm of service insignia consists of the number 64 in a horizontally divided red-over-yellow square on the hull front plate next to the NZ number, while the tank number B was painted in white inside a blue circle. It would be completed in overall Bronze Green. [P. McKay]

Valentines on manoeuvres at Waiouru in the 1950s. While the unit unknown they are notable for carrying crude tactical markings, the rear tank having the number 4 inside a C Squadron circle on the turret and on the ammunition box on the turret rear. They would have been completed in overall Bronze Green. [M. Priestly]

[Below left] A Valentine II (NZ16505) of 2 Troop, C Squadron, 3rd Armored Regiment at the Tekapo training area in 1955. The arm of service insignia consists of the number 64 in a horizontally divided red-over-yellow square on the hull front plate next to the NZ number, while the white tank number 2B was painted in white inside a blue circle. It would be completed in overall Bronze Green. [J. McKay]

[Below] A line up of Valentine Vs on the ranges at Waiouru in the 1950s. All are completed in overall Bronze Green. NZ20744 on the left has a B Squadron square on the turret (color unknown). The other two tanks are from A Squadron, the tank in the center, NZ16480, carrying the name "Achilles" and a white number 1 inside the A Squadron triangle, while the Valentine on the right, also from A Squadron, is named "Apollo". No unit markings are apparent on the front plate, though "Achilles" does carry its NZ number there. [M. Priestly]

Valentine V (NZ20767) of 1st Armored Regiment (Waikato). The unit serial 59 was carried in a red-over-yellow diagonally divided square (the diagonal division usually indicative [of] Regular Force units), along with [th]e Kiwi insignia. The tank would be [co]mpleted in overall Bronze Green. [Th]e unit serials of the rest of the 4th [Ar]mored Brigade were: Headquarters [4t]h Armored Brigade – 58; 2nd Ar[m]ored Regiment – 64; 4th Armored [R]egiment – 63. [M. Priestly]

[A]n immaculate Valentine V (NZ20769) [of] 1st Armored Regiment (Waikato) [du]ring a parade in Auckland in 1959. [Th]e vehicle is completed in overall [s]emi-gloss Bronze Green. The tactical [in]signia is the white 59 in a red-over-[y]ellow horizontally divided square [an]d a white Kiwi in a black square. [Auckland Institute and Museum]

Color Plates

A Valentine II of 7 Troop, B Squadron, 1st Battalion, 1st NZ Army Tank Brigade at Waiouru Camp in 1942. The vehicle is completed in a three-tone scheme of Dark Green over-painted with stripes of Dark Earth and Khaki Green. The unit insignia was consisted of 21 in a red square on the right side and the letter A on the left side. The B Squadron square and troop number on the turret were red. The name "Ngara" was white while T-32736 was light blue.

All color plates in this book (except the front cover) are reproduced to 1/35th scale

A Valentine II from 15 Troop, C Squadron, 1st Battalion, 1st NZ Army Tank Brigade at Helvetia Military Camp, Pukekohe in 1943. The vehicle is completed in a two-tone camouflage scheme of Dark Green over-painted with stripes of Dark Earth. The unit insignia consisted of the unit serial 21 in a red square on the right side of the front plate of the tank and Rampant Dragon in a black square on the left, while in between was the tactical insignia of a red 15 inside a red circle. This was repeated on the hull rear. The squadron insignia and troop number were also painted on both sides of the turret along with the name "Taniwha" in white (Taniwha was a Maori name for a mythical creature that lived in deep pools in rivers and dark caves or in the sea).

A Valentine V of C Squadron, 2nd Queen Alexandra's Mounted Rifles at the Wanganui racecourse in 1943. It is completed in overall S.C.C. 2 Brown and carries the 4th Division insignia, a charging water buffalo in a red square on the front and rear plates along with their unit serial 7 in a green square, the latter having been painted directly over the War Department serial so that only T-5 is visible. The C Squadron circle on the turret was green outlined in white.

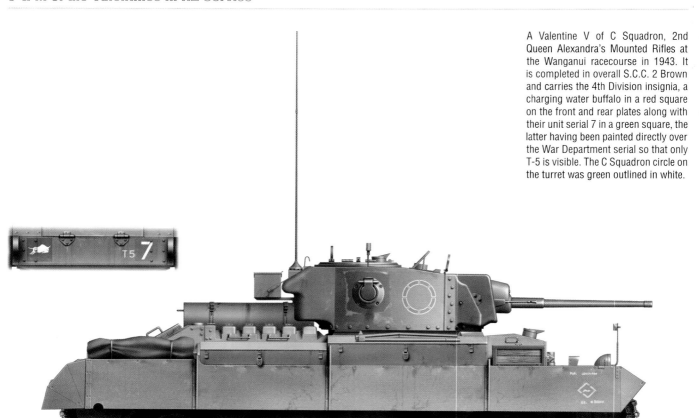

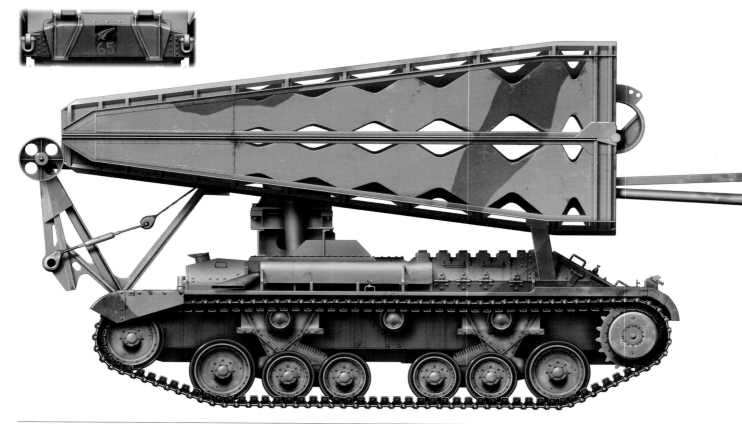

Above & below right A Valentine V from the Brigade Headquarters Squadron of the 1st NZ Army Tank Brigade at Harewood Camp in 1943. It is completed in a two-tone scheme of Dark Green and Dark Earth. The unit insignia consisted of the unit serial 20 in a brown square and the dragon in a black square. The Army number (NZ13905), name ("Sidi Barrani") and 4 in the triangular pennant insignia on the turret are white.

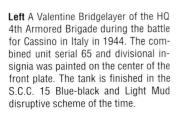

Left A Valentine Bridgelayer of the HQ 4th Armored Brigade during the battle for Cassino in Italy in 1944. The combined unit serial 65 and divisional insignia was painted on the center of the front plate. The tank is finished in the S.C.C. 15 Blue-black and Light Mud disruptive scheme of the time.

Below & bottom left The Squadron second in command's Valentine III CS from SHQ, 3rd NZ Division Tank Squadron on Nissan Island in February 1944. The tank is completed in a three-tone scheme of base color Khaki Green, over-painted on the upper surfaces with Dark Green and then over-sprayed with spots of Lime Green. The tactical insignia consisted of the unit serial 26 in a yellow square on the right side of the front plate, a Kiwi in a black square next to it, a yellow diamond with a white 2 in the center and the simplified Rampant Dragon insignia in a black square on the left side. The unit serial, Kiwi and Dragon insignia were repeated on the same side of the tank on the rear plate. The diamond and 2 were also found on both sides of the turret and on the rear Bren ammunition bin.